A Month with
Julian of Norwich

Edited by Rima Devereaux

spck

First published in Great Britain in 2018

Society for Promoting Christian Knowledge
36 Causton Street
London SW1P 4ST
www.spck.org.uk

British Library Cataloguing-in-Publication Data
A catalogue record for this book is available from the British Library

ISBN 978-0-281-07902-5
eBook ISBN 978-0-281-07903-2

Typeset by Fakenham Prepress Solutions, Fakenham, Norfolk NR21 8NN
Manufacture managed by Jellyfish
First printed in Great Britain by CPI
Subsequently digitally printed in Great Britain

eBook by Fakenham Prepress Solutions, Fakenham, Norfolk NR21 8NN

Produced on paper from sustainable forests

Introduction

Julian of Norwich (1343–1416) was an anchoress – someone set apart for God, living a life of solitary prayer and contemplation in a cell. Because the cell was usually attached to the parish church, an anchoress was involved in the issues of her day. Julian was attached to the church of St Julian in Norwich. We know from *The Book of Margery Kempe* that she was well known as a spiritual director. She advised many people who came to her, many of them, we can assume from the upheaval of those times, in a lot of pain.

Julian's book, the *Revelations of Divine Love*, from which these extracts are taken, is the first book in English known to have been written by a woman. It is the result of sixteen visions of Christ that she received in May 1373. These conveyed to her Jesus' passionate love for us and led her to compare it to a mother's love. Her writings are full of earthy details on the suffering of Jesus, which are rooted in medieval religious imagery, but these details are not gratuitous – they always guide us towards Jesus' compassion.

Julian's spirituality was refreshingly feminine and, characteristically, rejected both the institutional rigidity and the idea of the wrath of God that were common in her day: 'For two hundred years before Julian's birth, the Western Church had been moving towards ever more rigid, hierarchical, male-dominated, confrontational structures, culminating in catastrophic institutional stand-offs.'[1] Julian's God is, by contrast, one of mercy: 'According to her vision of God, he has always been present in everything, and has always been imparting unconditional love, but our own blindness has made this difficult to see.'[2] The life of Julian was rooted in the world and in the lives of the people who came to her cell's window for advice – and she ministers to us in a similar way across the centuries.

A Month with
Julian of Norwich

DAY

1

Morning

I thought I had some awareness of the Passion of Christ, but yet I desired more by the grace of God. I thought I would have liked to be at that time with Mary Magdalene, and with others that loved Christ, and therefore I desired an actual sight through which I might have more knowledge of the physical sufferings of our Saviour and of the compassion of our Lady and of all those who truly loved him and saw his sufferings at that time. For I wanted to be one of them and suffer with him. I never desired any other sight or shewing of God till the soul had departed from the body. The reason for this petition was that after the shewing I would have a more true awareness of the Passion of Christ.

Evening

And being in youth as yet, I thought it great sorrow to die; but for nothing earthly that I wished to live for, nor did I fear any pain: for I trusted in the mercy of God. But I wished to have lived in such a way that I might have loved God better . . . For I thought all the time that I had lived here so briefly and for so short a time in comparison to that eternal state of blessing . . . And so I thought: 'Good Lord, may the ending of my life be to your glory.' And I understood by my reason and by my painful suffering that I would die; and I surrendered my will completely to be in accord with God's will.

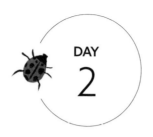

DAY

2

Morning

In this moment suddenly I saw the red blood trickle down from under the garland hot and fresh and copious, as it was in the time of his Passion when the garland of thorns was pressed on his blessed head who was both God and human, the same who suffered thus for me. I conceived truly and deeply that it was Christ himself who shewed it to me, without anyone in between.

And in the same shewing suddenly the Trinity filled my heart with utmost joy . . . For the Trinity is God: God is the Trinity; the Trinity is our Maker and Keeper, the Trinity is our everlasting love and everlasting joy and blessing, through our Lord Jesus Christ.

Evening

Also in this he shewed me a little thing, the quantity of an hazelnut, in the palm of my hand; and it was as round as a ball. I looked at it with the eye of my understanding, and thought: 'What is this?' And it was answered generally thus: 'It is all that is made.' I wondered how it might last, for I thought it might suddenly have fallen apart in dust as it was so small. And I was answered in my understanding: 'It lasts, and ever shall last because God loves it.' And so everything owes its existence to the love of God.

DAY
3

Morning

This shewing was made to teach our soul wisely to hold fast to the goodness of God. And in that time the method of our praying was brought to mind: how we tend, through lack of understanding and knowledge of God in his love, to spend too much time on petitioning him. Then saw I truly that it gives more honour to God, and more true delight, that we trustingly pray to him through his goodness and cling to him through his grace, with true confidence and in steadfast love, than if we took all the words that the heart can think. For if we use all these words, it is too little, and not truly worthy of God: but to rely on his goodness is all we need, and *there* nothing whatsoever is lacking.

Evening

I have not received this shewing because I am good; I am good only in so far as I love God deeply: and if you love God more deeply than I do, this shews you are better than I am. I tell this not to them that are wise, for they know it well; but I tell you that are simple, for ease and comfort: for we are all one in need of such comfort . . . For if I look only at myself, I am nothing at all; but in the general body I am, I hope, united in love with all my fellow Christians.

DAY
4

Morning

These are two workings that may be seen in this vision: the one is seeking, the other is seeing. The seeking is common – something every soul may do with his grace – and should be done with the care and teaching of the Holy Church. It is God's will that we do three things in our seeking: the first is that we seek earnestly and diligently, without sloth, and, as it may be through his grace, without too much weariness and useless gloom. The second is that we follow him steadfastly out of love for him, without grumbling and struggling against him, to our life's end: for life will always be short. The third is that we trust in him deeply in full assurance of faith.

Evening

Wherefore I need to acknowledge that whatever happens, happens for a reason: for it is our Lord God who causes it all. For at this time the working of creation itself was not shewn, but the working of our Lord God in what he has created: for he is the focal point of everything, and all that happens is due to him. And I was certain he does no sin. And here I saw truly that sin is not something that is done: for in all this sin was not shewn. And I needed no longer to marvel at this, but to watch our Lord, to see what he would shew. And thus, as much as could be understood for the time being, the righteousness of God's working was shewn to the soul.

DAY

5

Morning

On this shewed our Lord that the Passion of him is the overcoming of the devil. God shewed that the devil has now the same malice that he had before the incarnation. And struggle as he might, he still sees that all souls of salvation escape him, by the worth and virtue of Christ's precious Passion. And that is his sorrow, and shame comes to him: for all that God allows him to do turns for us to joy and for him to shame and woe . . . But . . . our good Lord endlessly has regard to the honour which is his due and to the benefit of all who shall be saved. With might and right he resists the enemy, who out of malice and wickedness occupies himself to contrive and to act against God's will.

Evening

And in this shewing my understanding was lifted up to heaven where I saw our Lord as a lord in his own house, who had called all his beloved servants and friends to a ceremonial feast. Then I saw the Lord occupied no place in his own house, but I saw him regally preside in his house, filling it with joy and happiness, himself endlessly ready to gladden and to cheer his beloved friends, full homely and full courteously, with a marvellous expression of endless love, in his own fair blessed countenance. This glorious countenance of the Godhead fills the heavens with joy and blessedness.

DAY

6

Morning

God shewed three measures of blessing that every soul who has willingly served God in any way on earth shall enjoy in heaven. The first is the most valuable thanks of our Lord God that a person shall receive when delivered from pain. This gratitude is so supremely worthwhile that the soul will feel it filled with it even if there were to be nothing more . . . The second is that all the blessed creatures that are in heaven shall see that worthy gratitude, as he makes that person's service known to all that are in heaven . . . The third is that, as new and as gladdening as it is received in that time, it will last in just the same way for evermore.

Evening

This vision was shewn me, as far as I could understand, because it is helpful to some souls to feel in this way: sometimes to be in comfort, and sometimes to fail and to be left to themselves. God wishes us to know that he keeps us equally secure in good times and in bad. And for the benefit of his soul, a person is sometimes left to struggle on alone . . . And both experiences are aspects of his divine love. For it is God's will that we maintain our strength with all that is within our power . . . And therefore it is not God's will that we follow the feelings of pain in sorrow and mourning for them, but that we suddenly rise above them and find ourselves in a place of eternal rejoicing.

DAY

7

Morning

The blessed body dried alone for a long time with the tearing of the nails and the weight of the body. For I understood that because the sweet hands and feet were so tender, due to the large size, sharpness and vicious shape of the nails the wounds opened wide and the body started to sag because it was heavier after hanging for so long. And the head was pierced and pressured by the crown of thorns, and the sweet hair, stiffened with dried blood, was stuck to the crown, and the thorns stuck to the drying skin; and at the beginning, while the flesh was newly bleeding, the continual pressure of the thorns made the wounds split open.

Evening

I thought: 'Is any pain like this?' And I was answered in my reason: 'Hell is another kind of pain: for there lies the pain of despair. But of all pains that lead to salvation this is the worst pain, to see your Lord suffer. How might any pain be worse for me than to see him that is all my life, all my bliss, and all my joy, suffer?' Here felt I sincerely that I loved Christ so much more than myself that there was no pain that could be felt like that sorrow that I had to see him in agony.

DAY

8

Morning

Then an idea came into my mind, as if it had been a friendly voice saying: 'Look up to heaven to his Father.' . . . Either I had to look up or else to answer. I answered inwardly with all the strength of my soul, and said: 'No; I cannot: for you are my heaven.' . . . Thus was I taught to choose Jesus as my heaven . . . I liked no other heaven than Jesus, who shall be my blessed fulfilment when I get there.

And this has ever been a comfort to me, that I chose Jesus as my heaven, by his grace, in all this time of Passion and sorrow; and that has been a teaching to me that I should evermore do so: choose only Jesus as my heaven in good times and bad.

Evening

For as long as he was able to suffer he did so: for our sake, he suffered for us and also lamented over us; and now he is risen and beyond all personal suffering, yet he still suffers *with* us.

And I, realizing all this through his grace, saw that his love was so strong which he has for our souls that willingly he chose to suffer with great desire, and humbly he was happy to do so. For when the soul that considers this is touched by grace, it shall truly see that the agonies of Christ's Passion surpass all other agonies: all sufferings, that is to say, which shall be turned into everlasting, supreme joys by the virtue of Christ's Passion.

DAY

9

Morning

I understood that we are now, in our Lord's meaning, at his cross with him in his suffering and his Passion, dying; and if we willingly hold on to the same cross with his help and his grace to the very end, then suddenly he shall turn his cheerful expression towards us, and we shall be with him in heaven. Between one state and the other there shall be no time, and then shall all be brought to joy. And thus said he in this shewing: 'Where is now any point of your suffering or your grief?' And we shall be deeply blessed.

Evening

And here saw I truly that if he shewed now to us his blessed countenance, there is no suffering on earth or anywhere else that could overcome us . . . But because he shews to us the time of his Passion, as he bore it in *this* life, and his cross, therefore we are in distress and hardship, with him, according to the measure of our own frailty. And the reason why he permits it to be so is because he will out of his goodness bring us closer to him in his blessedness; and for this trivial suffering that we experience here, we shall receive a high eternal understanding of God . . . And the heavier our sufferings have been with him on his cross, the more shall our glory be with him in his kingdom.

DAY
10

Morning

For it is God's will that we have true rejoicing with him in our salvation, and therein he wishes us to be deeply comforted and strengthened . . . For we are his blessing: for in us he rejoices for ever; and so shall we do in him, through his grace. And all that he has done for us, and does, and ever shall, was never a cost or a price to him, nor could ever be, but only in so far as what he did in his humanity, beginning at the sweet incarnation and lasting to the blessed resurrection on Easter morning: so long he endured the cost and the price to bring about our redemption and all the time he rejoiced throughout, as I have said before.

Evening

Then with a glad expression our Lord looked at his side and regarded it with joy. With his sweet looking he increased my understanding so that I, created by him, could also enter into his side. And then he shewed a fair, delightful place, and large enough for all humankind that shall be saved to rest in peace and in love. And in this way he brought to mind his beloved blood and precious water which he poured all out for love of us. And with his tender beholding he shewed me his blessed heart even riven in two.

DAY

11

Morning

And after this our Lord shewed himself more glorified, as I saw it, than I saw him before in the shewing wherein I was taught that our soul shall never have rest till it comes to him, knowing that he is fullness of joy, homely and courteous, blessed and our very life.

Our Lord Jesus frequently said: 'It is I, it is I, it is I who is the most exalted, it is I whom you love, it is I whom you rejoice in, it is I whom you serve, it is I whom you long for, it is I whom you desire, it is I whom you mean, it is I who is all. It is I about whom the Holy Church preaches and teaches you, it is I who shewed myself here to you.'

Evening

But I saw not sin itself, for I believe it has no actual substance or any measure of being, nor could it be known except through the suffering it brings. And likewise pain; this suffering, as I see it, has purpose for a time; for it purifies us, and makes us come to our senses and to ask for mercy. For the Passion of our Lord brings us comfort in the face of all this, for thus is his blessed will. And for the deep love that our good Lord has to all that shall be saved, he comforts us readily and tenderly, signifying thus: 'It is true that sin is the cause of all this pain; but all shall be well, and all shall be well, and all manner of thing shall be well.'

DAY

12

Morning

And then I saw that each instance of natural compassion that human beings feel for their fellow Christians with charity is Christ acting in them . . . In this were two manners of understanding what our Lord meant. One is the blessing that we are brought to . . . The other is for comfort in our pain: for he desires us to realize that this pain will be turned into glory and benefit by virtue of his Passion, and that we also realize that we suffer not alone but with him, and see him to be the ground of our being, and that we understand that his suffering and his abnegation surpass so far anything we may suffer that we shall never fully grasp it. The contemplation of this will save us from resentment and despair as we experience our sufferings.

Evening

One time our good Lord said: 'All thing shall be well'; and another time he said: 'You shall see, yourself, that all *manner* of thing shall be well'; and in these two sayings the soul understood different meanings. One was that he wishes us to know that he takes heed not only to noble things and to great, but also to little and to small, to low and to simple, to one and to another. And thus means he in that he says: '*All manner of thing* shall be well.' For he wishes us to know that the least thing shall not be forgotten.

DAY
13

Morning

Our faith is grounded in God's word . . . and one point of our faith is that many creatures shall be condemned: as angels that fell out of heaven for pride . . . and many on earth that die outside of the faith of Holy Church . . . and also many that have received Christendom and live unchristian lives . . . And understanding all this, I thought it was impossible that all manner of things should be well . . . And as to this I had no other answer in the shewing of our Lord God but this: 'That which is impossible to you is not impossible to me: I shall save my word in all things and I shall make all things well.'

Evening

Our Lord God shewed that a deed shall be done, and he himself shall do it, and I shall do nothing but sin, yet my sin shall not prevent his goodness from working. And I saw that the contemplation of this is a heavenly joy in a fearing soul which evermore sincerely by grace desires God's will. This deed shall be begun here, and it shall give glory to God and be abundantly beneficial to those who love him on earth; and ever as we come to heaven we shall see it in marvellous joy, and it shall last thus in working until the last day; and the glory and the blessing of it shall last in heaven before God and all his holy ones for ever.

DAY

14

Morning

God brought to my mind that I would still sin . . . And this shewing I regarded as being specifically meant for me; but by all the gracious comfort that follows, as you shall see, I was taught to take it as meaning all my fellow Christians: everyone in general and not any specific individual: although our Lord shewed me that I personally would sin it is to be understood that everyone would do so. And therein I conceived a creeping fear. And to this our Lord answered: 'I keep you utterly safely.' This word was said with more love and security and spiritual keeping than I can or may tell.

Evening

The reward that we shall receive shall not be trivial, but it shall be exalted, glorious and full of honour. And so shall shame be turned to honour and more joy. But our courteous Lord wills not that his servants despair, neither for frequent falling nor for serious: for our falling does not prevent him from loving us. Peace and love are ever in us, existing and active; but we are not always in peace and in love. But he desires that we take heed that he is the ground of our whole life in love; and furthermore that he is our everlasting Keeper and strongly defends us against our enemies, that are in hot pursuit and close behind us; and the more ground we give them by our falling, the more our need of him is.

DAY

15

Morning

This is an example of the royal friendship of our courteous Lord that he keeps us so tenderly while we are in a state of sin; and furthermore he touches us very gently and shews us our sin by the sweet light of mercy . . . And then are we stirred by the Holy Spirit through contrition to prayer and desire for the amending of our life . . . Then hope we that God has forgiven us our sins: and it is truth. And then shews our courteous Lord himself to the soul – well merrily and with glad cheer . . . saying sweetly thus: 'My darling, I am glad you have come to me: in all your misery I have ever been with you; and now you see my loving and we are united in blessedness.'

Evening

After this our Lord shewed me details concerning prayer, in which shewing I see two particular conditions necessary for prayer: one is righteousness, another is our complete trust. But yet often our trust is not complete: for we are not sure that God hears us, as we think because of our unworthiness, and because we feel nothing at all . . . And all this brought our Lord suddenly to my mind, and shewed these words, and said: 'I am the ground of your earnest seeking: first it is my will that you do pray; and after, I make you to want to; and after, I make you to pray in depth and you do pray in depth. How should it then be that you should not have what you earnestly seek?'

DAY
16

Morning

Our Lord God wills that we have true understanding of prayer, and specially in three things that belong to it. The first is: *by whom and how that our prayer arises. By whom*, he shews when he says: 'I am the ground'; and *how*, by his goodness: for he says first: 'It is my will.' The second is: *in what manner and how we should use our prayer*; and that is that our wills become more in tune with our Lord's will . . . The third is that we should know *the fruit and the result of our prayers*: that is, that we be united and like our Lord in all things . . . And he will help us, and we shall make it come to pass as he says himself. Blessed may he be!

Evening

For prayer is the right way to understand that fullness of joy that is to come, prayer in a spirit of deep longing and complete trust . . . It is necessary for us to do our duty with diligence; and even when we have done it, then shall we still think that it is nothing – and in truth it is nothing. But if we do what we can, and ask, in sincerity, for mercy and grace, all that we lack we shall find in him. And this is what he means when he says: 'I am the ground of your earnest seeking.' And thus in this blessed word, with the shewing, I saw a full overcoming of all our weakness and all our doubtful fears.

DAY
17

Morning

God judges us looking upon our essential being, which is ever kept one in him, whole and safe without end: and *this* judgement is because of his righteousness in which it is made and kept. And human beings judge according to the changeable sensitivities of our souls, which veer this way and that according to the vagaries of our mood – and this is what we show through our outward behaviour. And this wisdom of human judgement is confused because of the different things that catch its attention. For sometimes it is good and easy-going, and sometimes it is harsh and severe.

Evening

But our transitory life that we experience here in our feelings knows not what our real self is. And when we truly and clearly see and know what our real self is then shall we truly and clearly see and know our Lord God in fullness of joy . . . We may be aware of our true self in this life by the constant help and virtue of our high nature. In this awareness we may persevere and grow, by the advancement and benefit of mercy and grace; but we may never fully know our real self until our last breath: at this point this transitory life and degree of pain and suffering shall have an end.

DAY

18

Morning

I understand this: human beings are changeable in this life, and by frailty and ignorance fall into sin: they are weak and foolish, and also the human will is not strong enough. And at this time they fall prey to inner turmoil, sorrow and woe; and the reason is spiritual blindness: for they are no longer aware of God. For if they were continually aware of God, they would not be inclined towards mischief, nor towards any kind of temptation or craving that might lead them into sin. Thus saw I, and realized at the same time; and I thought that the insight and the realization were vivid and abundant and a gift of grace . . . but even so they seemed insignificant and trivial in comparison with the great desire that the soul has to see God.

Evening

But our good Lord the Holy Spirit, which is everlasting life and which dwells in our soul, keeps us in utter safety; and brings about a peace and serenity through grace, and aligns it to God and makes it docile . . . For I saw no anger apart from human anger; and that he forgives us for. For anger is nothing more than a perversion and an opposition to peace and love; and either it comes from a failing of strength, or a failing of wisdom, or a failing of goodness: these failings are not God's, but ours. For we through sin and wretchedness have in us a wretched and perpetual opposition to peace and love. And that shewed he to us so often in his loving gaze of concern and pity.

DAY

19

Morning

For I saw with utter certainty that wherever our Lord appears, there is total peace, and anger has no place. For I saw no degree of anger in God, either short-term or long-term; for in truth, as I saw it, if God was angry even for a moment, we should not survive in any degree whatsoever. For as truly as we owe our existence to the eternal almightiness of God and to his eternal wisdom and to his eternal goodness, so in the same way we owe our security to the eternal almightiness of God . . . For although we feel ourselves to be frail wretches, filled with discord and quarrels, yet are we held safely in all ways by the gentleness of God and by his humility, by his kindness and by his grace.

Evening

I saw two persons in bodily likeness . . . a Lord and a servant; and God gave me spiritual understanding of them. The Lord is sitting in state, at rest and in peace; the servant is standing before his Lord reverently, ready to do his Lord's will. The Lord looks upon his servant with deep love and delight, and gently he sends him to a certain place to do his will. The servant not only goes, but suddenly he sets off and runs in great haste . . . And suddenly he falls into a ravine, and is consequently badly hurt . . . And in all this I saw that his chief injury was his loss of strength, for he could not turn his face to look upon his loving Lord, which was in fact quite close to him.

DAY

20

Morning

All those of us that will be saved experience in ourselves while we live a surprising mixture of good and evil: we have in us our risen Lord Jesus, we have in us too the wretchedness and the mischief of Adam's fall, and death. By Christ we are steadfastly kept, and through his grace touching us we are given assurance of salvation. And by Adam's fall we feel we are so broken, in various ways by sins and sorrows, through which we are made spiritually blind, that we can scarcely take any comfort. But in our intention we rest in God, and faithfully trust in his mercy and grace; and this is God's own working in us.

Evening

For God looks at things in one way and humankind looks at things in another. For it is natural for us to accuse ourselves in humility, and it is natural for the proper goodness of our Lord God to excuse us in courtesy. And these are two sides that were shewed in the twofold manner of regard with which the Lord beheld the falling of his beloved servant. The one was shewed outwardly, very kindly and tenderly . . . And this is how our Lord wills that we accuse ourselves, earnestly and truly seeing and knowing our falling and all the harm that comes thereof; seeing and learning that we by ourselves can never undo it; and in this way we earnestly and truly see and know his everlasting love for us.

DAY

21

Morning

For I saw that God never *began* to love humankind: for just as humankind will live in an eternal state of blessedness, delighting God with regard to his creation, so in the same way humankind has always been in the forefront of the mind of God: known and loved from all eternity in his righteous purpose. By the eternal assent and full agreement of all the Trinity, the Second Person willed to become the foundation and head of this lovely human nature: out of whom we have all come, in whom we are all enclosed, to whom we shall all go, in him finding our full heaven in everlasting joy, by the foreseeing purpose of all the blessed Trinity before time began.

Evening

We ought to rejoice greatly that God dwells in our soul, and we should rejoice even more that our soul dwells in God. Our soul is *made* to be God's dwelling-place; and the dwelling-place of the soul is God, which is *unmade*. And it calls for deep understanding, inwardly to see and know that God, which is our Maker, dwells in our soul; and an even deeper understanding is needed, inwardly to see and to know that our soul, that is made, dwells in God's substance: of that substance, God, we are what we are.

DAY

22

Morning

And all the gifts that God can give to his creation, he has given to his Son Jesus for us: and these gifts he, dwelling within us, has kept safe in himself until the time when we have developed and matured – our soul with our body and our body with our soul, each of them taking help from the other – till we are brought to a state of maturity, as nature forms us. And then, in the ground of nature, the Holy Spirit's merciful and gracious assistance breathes into us such gifts as will bring us to everlasting life.

Evening

God is nearer to us than our own soul: for he is the ground in which our soul is planted, and he is the means by which our essential being and our physical nature hold together so that they shall never be separated. For our soul sits in God its true rest, and is planted in God its true strength, and is intrinsically rooted in God in everlasting love: and therefore if we wish to know more about our soul, and connect with it and enjoy it, it is necessary to seek our Lord God in whom it is enclosed.

DAY

23

Morning

The wonderful city where our Lord Jesus sits is our physical nature, in which he is enclosed, while our essential being is enclosed in him – the blessed soul of Christ sits at rest in the Godhead. And I saw with utter certainty that we have to live in longing and repentance until the time when we are led so deeply into God that at last we really and truly do know our own soul. And I saw definitely that our Lord himself leads us into these mystical depths in the same love with which he created us and redeemed us by mercy and grace through the virtue of his blessed Passion.

Evening

I saw that in God our nature is complete: in which whole nature of humanness he makes different expressions of it flow out from him . . . he keeps our nature safe, and mercy and grace restore and make perfect. And of these none shall be lost: for our nature that is the higher part was united to God, at the creation; and God was united to our nature that is the lower part, when he was incarnate: and thus in Christ our two natures become one. For Christ is included in the Trinity . . . For I saw with utter certainty that all the works that God has done, or ever shall, were fully known to him and foreseen from before time began. And out of love he made humankind, and out of the same love he willed to become human himself.

DAY

24

Morning

Therefore our Lady is our Mother in whom we are all enclosed and of her born, in Christ (for she that is Mother of our Saviour is Mother of all that shall be saved in our Saviour): and our Saviour is our true Mother in whom we are eternally upheld, and we will never be separated from him . . . For it is his good pleasure to reign blessedly in our intellect, and sit in our soul at peace, and to dwell there for ever, weaving us all into him: and while this continues he desires us to be his helpers, giving to him all our attention, learning his lessons, keeping his laws, wanting us to do all that he does; truly trusting in him. For in truth I saw that our essential being is in God.

Evening

And thus is Jesus our true Mother by nature, by virtue of our first creation; and he is also our true Mother by grace, through taking our human nature. All the loving activity, and all that is implicit in the notion of the very best kind of motherhood has been appropriated to the Second Person . . .

I understood that there are three ways of looking at the motherhood in God: the first is rooted in the fact of our nature's *making*; the second is his *taking* of our nature – and this is the start of the motherhood of grace; the third is that motherhood of *working* – and in this activity the same grace is spread forth all over everything, everlasting in its length and breadth and height and depth. And this all springs from his one love.

DAY

25

Morning

The kind, loving mother that understands and knows the needs of her child nurtures it with great tenderness, according to the nature and condition of motherhood. And as the child grows older, she changes her methods but not her love. And when the child grows older still, she allows it to be chastised so that the child's faults are corrected and its virtues and graces are encouraged. By these actions, with others that are right and good, is our Lord at work in those who are doing these things: thus he is our Mother in nature by working grace in our lower part for the sake of our higher part.

Evening

God in his being is natural: that is to say, that what there is of goodness in nature is essentially of God. He is the substance, he is the very essence of nature. And he is the true Father and the true Mother of all natural creation: and every natural thing that he has made to flow out of him to fulfil his will shall be restored and brought back to him when humankind has been saved through the work of grace. For of all the natures that God has implanted to some extent in different creatures, he has implanted them completely in human beings; in wholeness and virtue, in beauty and goodness, in royalty and nobility, in all aspects of majesty, in value and glory.

DAY

26

Morning

Thus in our true Mother, Jesus, our life has been grounded through the foreseeing wisdom of himself from before time began, with the rich power of the Father, and the deep sovereign goodness of the Holy Spirit . . . And I understood that there is no higher state in this life than childhood, with its frailty and lack of strength in mind and body, until the time that our gracious Mother brings us up to our Father's state of blessedness in heaven. And then we will truly understand what he meant in those lovely words he spoke: 'All shall be well: and you shall see, yourself, that all manner of thing shall be well.' And then shall the blessedness of our motherhood in Christ be renewed to begin in the joys of our God.

Evening

And in these words: 'Suddenly you will be taken', I saw that God rewards us for the patience that we show in waiting for God's will, and for God's time, and for extending that patience to last throughout our lives. For ignorance as to the time of death brings great benefit: for if we knew our time of passing, our patience would not last; but it is the will of God that while the soul is in the body it should always feel as though it is at the point of being taken. For all this life and this languishing that we endure on earth last but a moment, and when we are taken suddenly out of suffering into blessing then the suffering will be as if it had never been.

DAY

27

Morning

And when we fall again into weariness, and spiritual blindness, and feelings of pain both spiritual and physical as a result of our weakness, it is God's will that we know that he has not forgotten us . . .

It is God's will that we take his promises and his consolations as generously and as wholeheartedly as we can, and also he wills that we take our waiting and our discomforts as lightly as we can, and think nothing of them. For the more lightly we take them, and the less value we place on them, for the love of God, the less pain we shall feel, and the more thanks and reward we shall receive.

Evening

And thus I understood that those who deliberately choose God in this life, out of love for him, can be sure that they are loved for ever and ever: and this eternal love of God comes to them by grace. For he wants us to be as certain in our hope of the blessings of heaven while we are here on this earth, as we shall be in perfect faith when we are actually there. And the more pleasure and joy that we take in this certainty, with reverence and humility, the more he is pleased, as it was shewed.

DAY

28

Morning

And then our Lord opened my spiritual eyes and shewed me my soul in the middle of my heart . . . And its area and surroundings shewed me that it was a most glorious city. In the middle of that city sat our Lord Jesus, God and human, a beautiful Person of great stature, the chief of bishops, the most stately King, the worthiest of all lords; and I saw him clothed in solemn majesty . . . And the Godhead rules and sustains heaven and earth and all that is – sovereign power, sovereign wisdom and sovereign goodness – but the place that Jesus occupies in our soul he will never leave again, never, as far as I see it: for in us is he totally at home and in us is his everlasting dwelling.

Evening

Thus I understood in very truth that our soul can never find its rest in things that are less than itself. And when it rises above all earthly things to its true self, yet it cannot live just by gazing at itself, but its total gaze must be blessedly fixed on God the Maker dwelling therein. For in our soul is God's true dwelling; and the most dazzling light and the brightest shining of the city is, as I see it, the glorious love of our Lord . . . And he wills that our hearts be exalted above the depths of the earth and all empty sorrows, and rejoice in him.

DAY
29

Morning

And these words: 'You will not be overcome' were said decisively and with great emphasis, for reassurance and comfort against all troubles that may come to us. He said not: 'You will not be caught up in storms, you will not be overstretched, you will not be made to suffer'; but he said: 'You will not be overcome.' God desires us to pay careful attention to these words, and for us to be ever strong in certain faith, in good times and bad. For he loves us and rejoices in us, and so it is his will that we love him and rejoice in him and put our deepest trust in him; and *all shall be well*.

Evening

God shewed that we have two kinds of spiritual sickness: the first is impatience or sloth, because we make such heavy weather of our hardships and suffering; the second is despair or a doubting fear, of which I am about to speak . . . And these two are they that cause most trouble and upset us, as our Lord shewed me; and these are the ones he wishes us to amend . . . For it is through our spiritual blindness and physical laziness that we are most inclined towards these sins. And therefore it is God's will that we recognize them, for then we shall turn away from them as we do from other sins.

DAY
30

Morning

It is his will that we should know and understand four things: the first is that he is our ground in which we have all our life and our existence. The second is that he keeps us safe with his strength and mercy whenever we fall into sin or fall into the hands of our enemies, who are ready to destroy us; and we are in so much more danger because we give them the opportunity, not realizing our own need. The third is how courteously he protects us, and shews us when we are straying. The fourth is how loyally he waits for us and his concern never lessens: for he wants us to turn back to him again, and be united to him in love as he is to us.

Evening

And when we do fall, because we are weak or blind, then our courteous Lord touches us and encourages us and calls us; and then he wants us to realize our wretchedness and humbly take note of it. But he does not want us to remain in this state, nor does he want us to fret over our self-accusation, nor is it his will that we despair over ourselves; but he does want us to turn back to him with all speed. For he stands all alone and awaits us in sorrow and grief till we approach, and then he is quick to welcome us. For we are his joy and his delight, and he is our medicine and our life.

DAY 31

Morning

Our good Lord shewed himself to me in various ways, both in heaven and on earth, but I saw him make no dwelling except in the human soul. He shewed himself on earth in the sweet incarnation and in his blessed Passion . . . And in another way he shewed himself on earth as though he were on pilgrimage: that is to say, he is here with us, leading us, and shall be till the time when he has brought us all to his blessed state in heaven. He shewed himself on many occasions reigning, as I have said before; but principally in the human soul. He has made there his resting-place and his glorious city: from this glorious abode he will never rise nor abandon it for eternity.

Evening

And from that time when all this was shewed first, I often desired to see clearly what our Lord really meant. And more than fifteen years later, I was answered in my spiritual understanding, when I heard a voice: 'Do you wish to see clearly what your Lord means in this? Know it well: love was his meaning. Who shewed it to you? Love. What did he shew you? Love. Why did he shew it? For love. Hold on to this and you will learn and understand even more about love. But you will never know or learn anything else – not ever.'

Notes and source

Notes

1   A. N. Wilson, 'Introduction', in Julian of Norwich,
    Revelations of Divine Love, translated by Grace Warrack,
    modernized by Yolande Clarke (London: SPCK, 2017),
    p. xi.
2   Janina Ramirez, *Julian of Norwich: A Very Brief History*
    (London: SPCK, 2016), p. 46.

Source

Julian of Norwich, *Revelations of Divine Love*, translated
by Grace Warrack, modernized by Yolande Clarke, with an
Introduction by A. N. Wilson (London: SPCK, 2017). Here are
the page numbers from which the readings are taken:

Day 1: Morning, p. 4; Evening, p. 6
Day 2: Morning, p. 10; Evening, p. 12
Day 3: Morning, p. 14; Evening, p. 22

Day 4: Morning, p. 29; Evening, pp. 32–3
Day 5: Morning, pp. 40–1; Evening, p. 44
Day 6: Morning, pp. 44–5; Evening, p. 49
Day 7: Morning, p. 54; Evening, p. 56
Day 8: Morning, pp. 59–60; Evening, p. 62
Day 9: Morning, pp. 63–4; Evening, p. 64
Day 10: Morning, pp. 69–70; Evening, p. 72
Day 11: Morning, p. 80; Evening, p. 82
Day 12: Morning, p. 85; Evening, p. 92
Day 13: Morning, pp. 93–4; Evening, p. 101
Day 14: Morning, p. 104; Evening, p. 109
Day 15: Morning, p. 110; Evening, p. 114
Day 16: Morning, p. 117; Evening, p. 119
Day 17: Morning, p. 126; Evening, p. 128
Day 18: Morning, pp. 131–2; Evening, p. 134
Day 19: Morning, pp. 136–7; Evening, pp. 141–2
Day 20: Morning, p. 154; Evening, pp. 156–7
Day 21: Morning, p. 159; Evening, p. 161
Day 22: Morning, p. 164; Evening, pp. 166–7
Day 23: Morning, p. 167; Evening, pp. 169–70
Day 24: Morning, p. 171; Evening, pp. 176–7
Day 25: Morning, p. 180; Evening, pp. 184–5
Day 26: Morning, pp. 187–8; Evening, p. 190
Day 27: Morning, p. 192; Evening, p. 193
Day 28: Morning, p. 200; Evening, p. 201
Day 29: Morning, p. 203; Evening, pp. 213–14
Day 30: Morning, p. 227; Evening, p. 230
Day 31: Morning, p. 233; Evening, p. 241